ABC's
OF THE
OCEAN

ISAAC ASIMOV

WALKER & COMPANY
New York

First published in the United States of America in 1970 by Walker and Company, a division of the Walker Publishing Company, Inc.

Published simultaneously in Canada by The Ryerson Press, Toronto

Library of Congress Catalog Card Number: 75-126120

ISBN: Trade 0-8027-6086-4; Reinforced 0-8027-6087-2

Printed in the United States of America

Book designed by Lena Fong Hor

ACKNOWLEDGMENTS

The publisher is grateful for permission to use the following photographs and illustrations

Air France
Page 25 (left)

ALCOA
Page 26

The American Museum of Natural History
Pages 9, 17, 20, 21, 22, 25 (right), 29,
34 (left), 35 (left), 37, 43, 44, 45, 47, 48 (right)

BLH Corporation
Page 11

Bureau of Commercial Fisheries, U.S. Department of the Interior
Pages 15, 24 (right), 31, 35 (right), 48 (left)

Canadian National Film Board
Page 13

Dr. Marie P. Fish, Narragansett Marine Laboratory
Page 19

General Dynamics (U.S. Nautilus)
Page 28

General Electric Company, Space Technology Center
Page 38

Lena Fong Hor
Pages 30, 32

Jamaica Tourist Board (Port Antonio)
Page 42 (right)

Matthew Kalmenoff
Pages 5, 14, 18, 27, 34 (right), 36, 40, 41, 42 (left)

The Kelco Company
Page 24 (left)

Marineland of Florida
Page 33

New Brunswick Travel Bureau, Canada
Page 7

Peabody Museum, Salem, Massachusetts ("Hurricane")
Page 46

U.S. Army Corps of Engineers
Page 23

U.S. Coast Guard
Page 6

U.S. Navy
Pages 4, 10

TO BEN BOVA AND HARRY STUBBS,

FRIENDS AND COLLEAGUES

A is for Aquanaut

a person who works
underwater, sometimes
for weeks. He lives in
special air-filled rooms, as
deep as fifty feet under the
ocean surface, and also
explores outside. "Aqua"
is the Latin word for water,
so any word that begins
with it has something to do
with water. "Naut" is from
the Greek word that means
sailor.

4

a is for aquaculture

_____
_____
_____

farming the sea. Fish and shellfish are raised in protected places in the ocean so there will be more of them to eat. New kinds of food are studied and grown. Men will be eating more different foods from the sea in days to come. Seaweed and tiny sea animals will probably be some of them.

B is for Buoy

_____

_____

a floating object, anchored to the bottom, to mark a place in the water. It might mark a rock to avoid, or water deep enough for boats to sail through. Some buoys are tall and thin, some short and thick. Some have a bell or a whistle attached, which the waves set off to warn boatmen. Some have a flag or a light for the same purpose.

6

b is for bore

_____

_____

_____

a high-breaking wave that moves upstream from the mouth of a river. The force of the moon pulls the ocean water. In some places, water is pulled from the ocean into a river mouth. There is a river in China in which the bore is fifteen feet high and moves as fast as a racehorse can run.

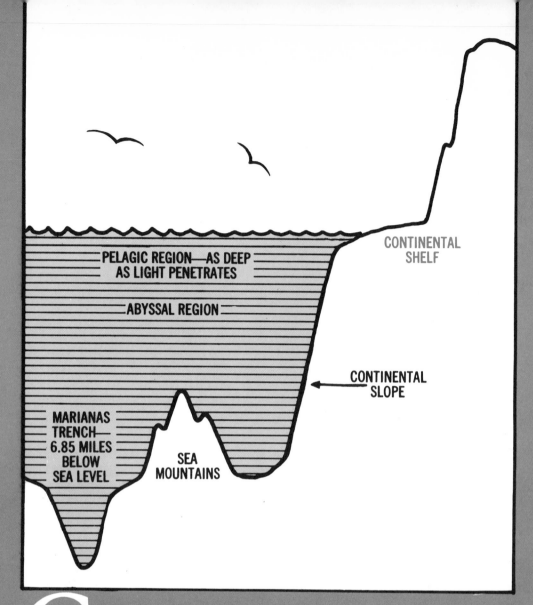

CONTINENTAL SHELF

PELAGIC REGION—AS DEEP
AS LIGHT PENETRATES

ABYSSAL REGION

CONTINENTAL
SLOPE

MARIANAS
TRENCH—
6.85 MILES
BELOW
SEA LEVEL

SEA
MOUNTAINS

C is for Continental Shelf

the part of the ocean bottom near a continent. It is flat and not very deep. Sometimes it runs out for a hundred miles. It gradually gets deeper and finally comes to a sharp drop. Almost all the fish we eat are caught in the waters over the Continental Shelf.

C is for current

_____

_____

_____

a flow of water across the top of the ocean, or
sometimes deep down in it. The ocean water warms
up in the tropics and spreads out into colder regions.
That makes the current, which moves around the
edges of the ocean. The Gulf Stream is a current of
warm water which flows north along the eastern coast
of the United States, then east toward northern
Europe.

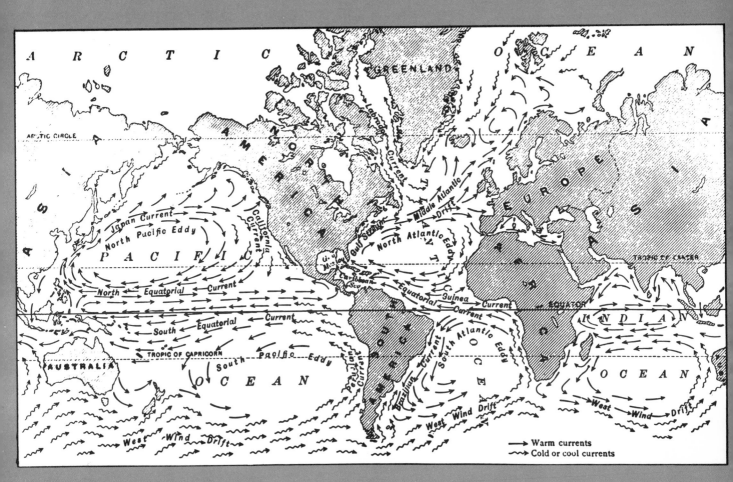

D is for Dragon's Tail

_____

_____

_____

an instrument called a thermistor, which is pulled
behind a ship by a long chain. It takes the ocean's
temperature to be recorded aboard the ship. Changes
in water temperature help us understand how currents
of water move about in the ocean.

d is for desalination

_____

_____

_____

turning salt water into fresh water. The sun does this
when its heat draws water from the ocean, leaving the
salt behind. Then the water turns into vapor, or mist,
that forms clouds. When the clouds turn into rain,
we get fresh water. Because fresh water is becoming
scarce, it is important to find ways of taking salt out
of sea water.

E is for Echo Sounding

a way of measuring the depth of the ocean by sound.
The sound is sent downward, hits bottom, and comes
back up. From the time it takes scientists to hear the
echo, they can tell how far the sound traveled and how
deep the ocean is there. This is because they know
the speed that sound travels through the sea water.

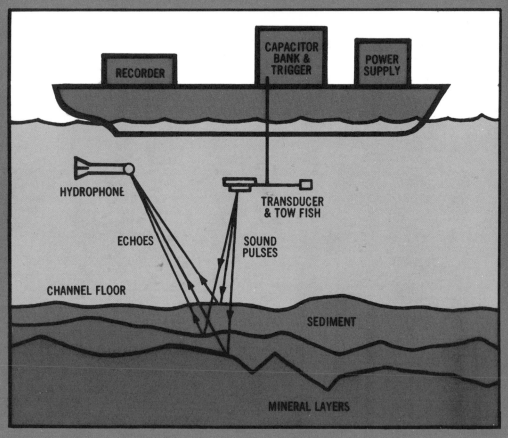

Echo Sounding

e is for ebb tide

_____

_____

_____

the movement of the ocean away from the shore. The moon's force causes the ocean water to rise and fall. That makes the water move onto the land and then back out again. The rising and falling are the tides. At its highest, the water is at flood tide. As it gets lower, it is ebb tide. About every twelve hours there is a high tide, and twelve hours later there is a low tide. This happens all over the world.

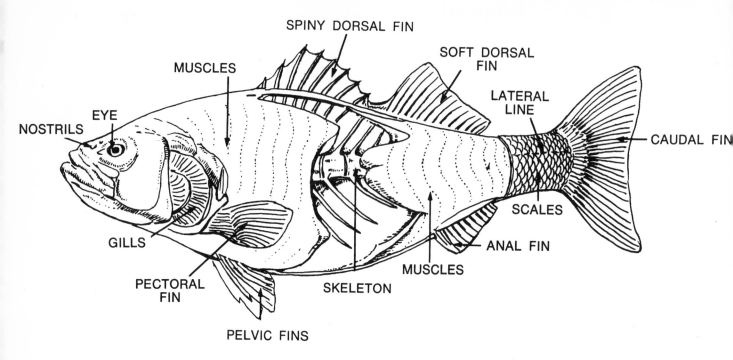

SPINY DORSAL FIN

MUSCLES

SOFT DORSAL FIN

LATERAL LINE

NOSTRILS EYE

CAUDAL FIN

GILLS

SCALES

PECTORAL FIN

ANAL FIN

MUSCLES

SKELETON

PELVIC FINS

F is for Fish

_____

_____

_____

animals that live underwater. They have bones inside their
bodies as we do, but they don't breathe air. Instead of
lungs they have gills that use the oxygen from the air
which is mixed with the water. There are thousands of
different kinds of fish. Many of them are good to eat, but
some are poisonous. Some glow in the dark. There is one,
the electric ray, that can give an electric shock when it

14 is touched.

f is for frogman

_____
_____
_____

a person who swims under water. He wears a rubber
suit. Rubber fins on his feet make it easier to get
around. A face mask keeps water out of his eyes. Air
is brought to his nose through tubes from a tank on
his back. He can observe fish where they live. He can
also explore old shipwrecks and the whole underwater
world.

G is for Guyot (GHEE-oh)

_____

_____

_____

an underwater mountain
with a flat top that once
rose above the ocean's
surface. After the top was
worn flat by waves, the
mountain slowly sank. A
guyot is also called a
seamount or a tablemount.

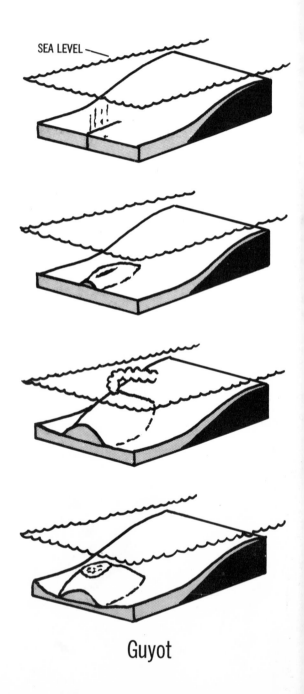

SEA LEVEL

Guyot

16

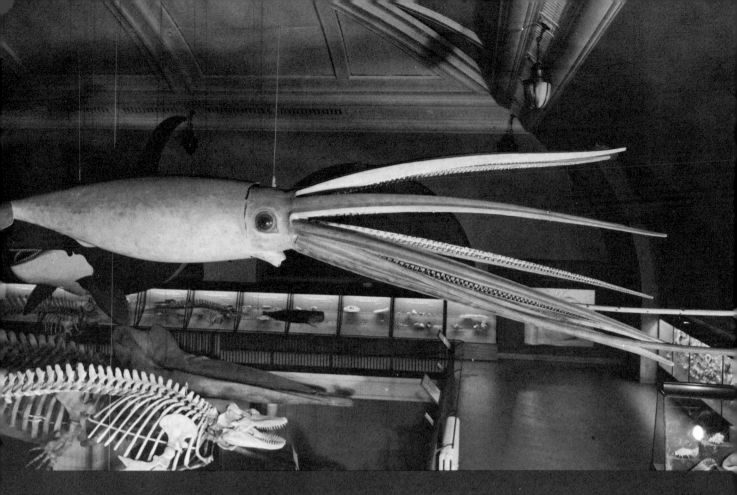

g is for giant squid

_____

_____

a large, boneless creature that lives at medium depths of the ocean. Its body can be ten feet long. It has ten arms. Two of them, the tentacles, can be fifty feet long. The other eight have sucking disks that can hold onto anything they touch. The squid is one of the fastest creatures in the sea. It moves by squirting out a jet of water like a rocket exhaust.

H is for Hadal

_____

_____

_____

a word for the most mysterious part of the ocean, the
deepest part, called trenches. The trenches are near
the edges of continents and along chains of islands. The
deepest known part of the ocean is 6.85 miles in the
southern end of the Marianas Trench. Water more than
three miles deep is the hadal region.

h **is for hydrophone**

_____

_____

_____

an instrument that picks up sounds from under water
so that scientists can listen to them. Living creatures
in the sea are as noisy as land creatures. They click,
squeak, whistle, and make other strange sounds.

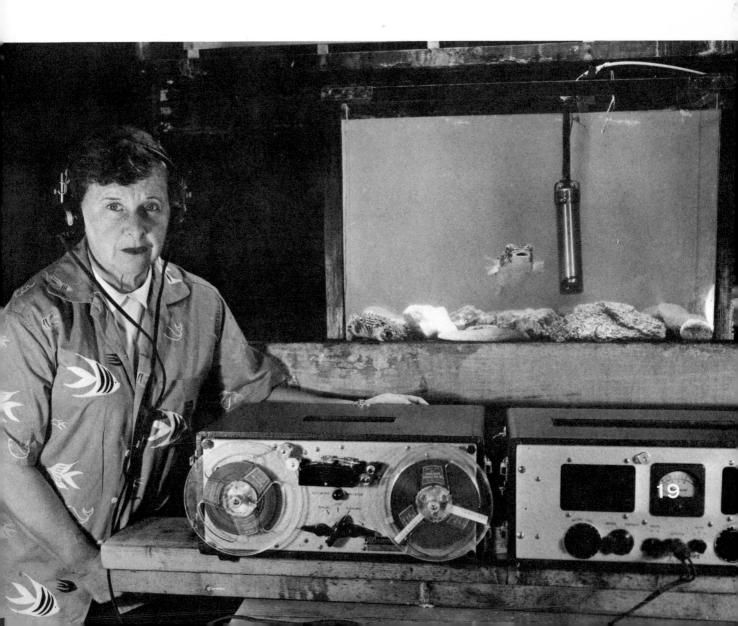

I is for Ichthyologist (ik-thee-OL-o-jist)

_____

_____

_____

a scientist who studies fish and everything about them. He—or she—might study the different kinds of fish which live today, or ancient kinds that no longer exist. He might be interested in where fish live, or in how to use them better to increase the world's food supply. "Ichthyo" comes from a Greek word for fish, and "logist" means a person who studies.

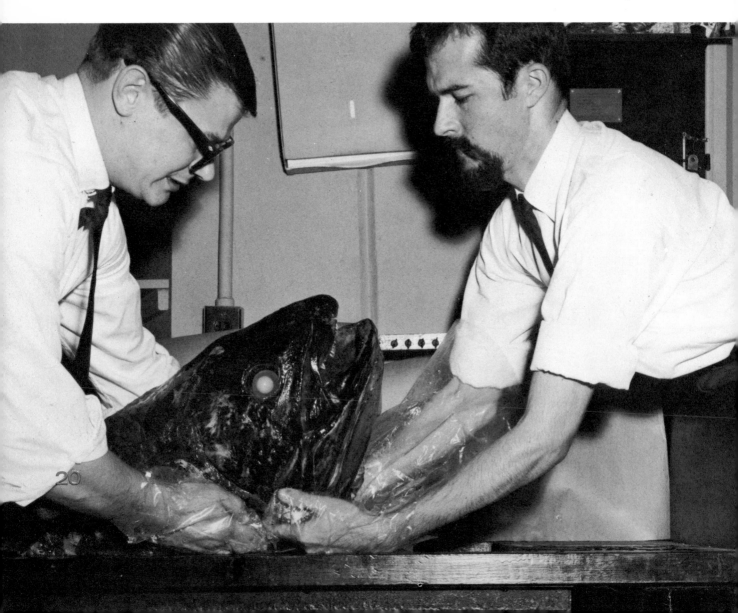

i is for iceberg

_____

_____

a huge block of ice which has broken off the ice of Greenland or Antarctica. Ocean currents carry icebergs into warmer seas where they slowly melt. Only a very small part of an iceberg—about one-tenth—sticks out above the water. The oceans must be carefully watched for icebergs. Collision with one can sink even a very big ship.

J is for Jellyfish

_____
_____
_____

a very simple form of ocean life. Jellyfish bodies look like masses of jelly shaped like umbrellas. All around the edges are stinging tentacles, or arms. These stun small sea creatures, which the jellyfish then eat. Most jellyfish are small, but the sun jellyfish can be eight feet wide and have tentacles 120 feet long. The Portuguese man-of-war is the most deadly and can kill a man.

22

j is for jetsam

_____

_____

_____

material thrown overboard to lighten a ship that is going down. Jetsam usually drops to the ocean bottom, but sometimes it is washed ashore. Material that floats after it is thrown overboard is called flotsam.

K is for Kelp

brown seaweed that is often very large. It grows in shallow parts of the ocean. Some kinds are attached to the ocean floor. Some float on the surface. Kelp collects minerals from the ocean water. When kelp is burned, the ashes are a valuable source of those minerals. Some day seaweeds will be used more widely as food. Already the Japanese grow some for this purpose. Seaweeds are used in medicine, too.

k is for krill

small shrimplike animals, usually about three inches long. They exist in great numbers in colder parts of the ocean, especially near Antarctica. Huge whales live on tiny krill. They scoop them up in their large mouths by the hundred thousand and eat them by the ton.

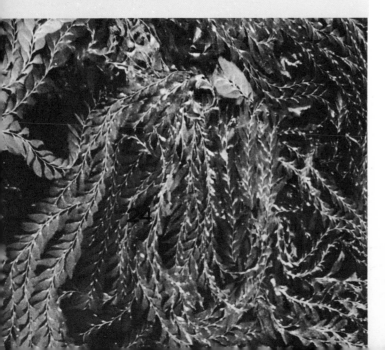

L is for Lagoon

a shallow bit of ocean that is nearly surrounded by land. The land protects it from the storms of the sea. Ships can find shelter in lagoons. It is safer to swim in the quiet water of a lagoon than in the open ocean.

l is for littoral

the stretch of shore between high tide and low tide. This land is covered with ocean water part of the time, and is bare part of the time. It has more different kinds of plants and animals than any other part of the ocean.

25

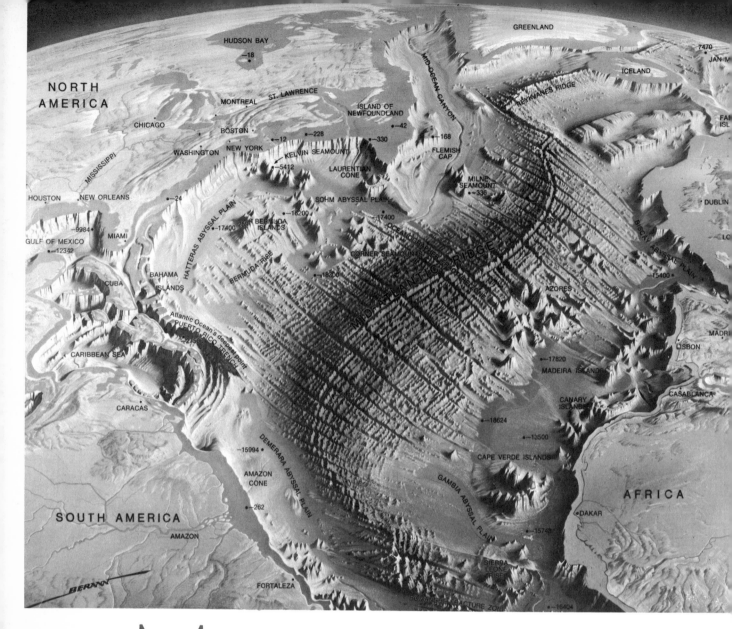

M is for Mid- oceanic Ridge

_____

_____

_____

the largest mountain range on earth. It was discovered by
echo sounding not long ago. It is almost entirely covered
by water, so men did not know it was there. It runs down

the middle of the Atlantic Ocean and around into the
Pacific Ocean and Indian Ocean, too. Part of it is higher
than the Rocky Mountains.

m is for marine snow

_____

_____

_____

specks of rock and living forms of life near the surface of the ocean. When they drift down in great numbers, they look like snow to divers underwater. Some tiny animals deep in the ocean live on marine snow. It is absorbed by sea plants, too. It helps to keep things alive all the way to the bottom of the ocean.

27

N is for Nuclear Submarine

_____

_____

_____

an underwater ship that gets its power from exploding atoms, or nuclear energy. An ordinary submarine must come to the surface to charge the batteries on which it runs, but a nuclear submarine can stay under water for months at a time. Nuclear submarines have explored the Arctic Ocean beneath the ice and have studied underwater mountain ranges.

n is for nautilus

a shellfish whose spiral shell is divided into separate sections, or chambers. Each section is bigger than the one behind. The nautilus forms them as it grows, and lives in the newest, biggest one. The outgrown chambers are filled with air and help the creature float. The first nuclear submarine was named "Nautilus."

29

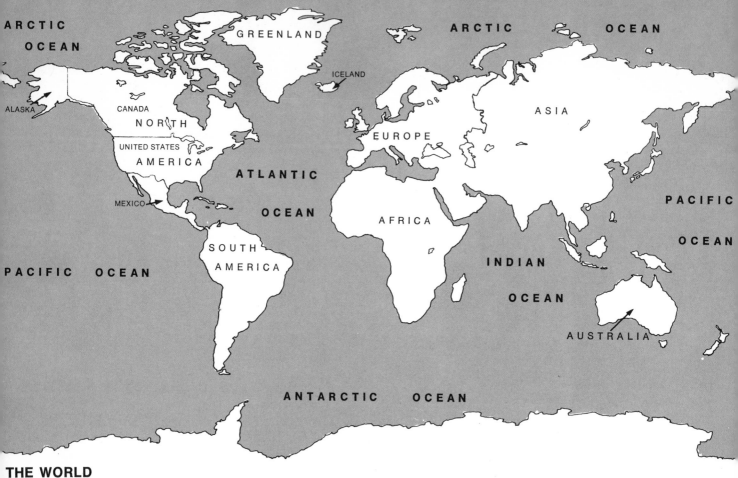

THE WORLD

O is for Ocean

_____

_____

_____

all of the salt water that covers almost three-quarters
of the earth's surface. We refer to different parts of
it by special names, such as the Atlantic Ocean, the
Pacific Ocean, or the Indian Ocean. But all are
connected. Sometimes the word sea is used instead
of ocean.

30

O is for oceanography

the scientific study of everything about the ocean. Many sciences are used in oceanography. Men and women study waves and water currents and tides. They study how sound and light travel under water. They study the different chemicals and minerals that are in ocean water. They examine the soil and the rocks at the bottom of the ocean, and the plants and animals that live there.

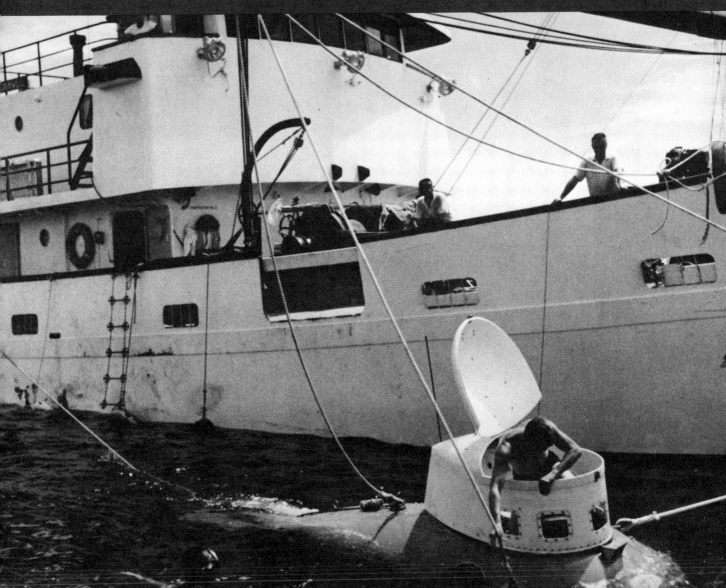

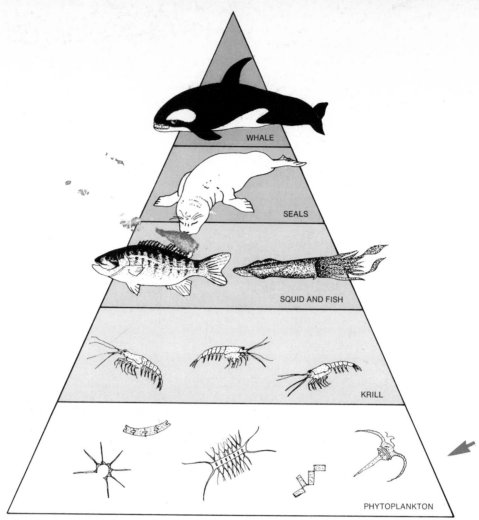

PYRAMID OF OCEAN LIFE

P is for Phytoplankton (fie-to-PLANGK-ton)

_____

_____

_____

tiny plants that float on the ocean surface. There are

trillions of them. They use the energy of sunlight to make

their food from air and water, and they give off oxygen.

Other forms of water life feed on phytoplankton, or on

forms of life that have earlier fed on phytoplankton.

"Phyto" comes from a Greek word that means plant, and

"plankton" comes from one meaning to wander or drift.

P is for porpoise

_____

_____

_____

an air-breathing creature that lives entirely in water. It is shaped like a fish and has flippers, but it is a mammal which has warm blood and lungs like human beings. It must come to the surface to breathe. Porpoises are about four to six feet long. They and their relatives, the dolphins, have large brains and seem to be very intelligent. Other mammals of the sea are whales, seals, sea leopards, sea elephants, walruses, sea otters, and sea cows.

Q is for Quartz

_____
_____
_____

one of the most common minerals of the earth's crust. Sometimes it is found as transparent crystals, clear as glass. White sand on the seashore is made up of tiny pieces of quartz which has been ground down by waves. The mud that covers the ocean floor has more quartz in it than any other mineral.

MOON

q is for quadrature

_____
_____
_____

HORIZON

SUN

34   the position when the moon and the sun are at right angles to one another. When either of them is high in the sky and the other is on the horizon, they are in quadrature.

R is for Reef

a line of rocky material that lies at or near the surface of the ocean. Reefs can be built of rocks, sand, or the skeletons of corals. A ring-shaped reef around shallow water is called an atoll. Sometimes a reef follows the line of a continent. The world's largest coral reef runs for 1,250 miles along the coast of Australia. It is called the Great Barrier Reef.

r is for red tide

a reddish color that sometimes spreads over the ocean surface. It occurs when microscopic reddish-brown plants multiply so much that they cover a large area of the water. When they die, a poison is given off which kills many sea creatures.

35

SARGASSO SE.

S is for Sargasso Sea

a section of the North Atlantic Ocean. The water currents around it move in a fast circle, leaving the Sargasso Sea at the calm center. A great deal of seaweed floats on it. The first person to pass through it was Columbus on his voyage to America.

S is for salina (sa-LIE-na)

_____

_____

_____

a stretch of salty, swampy water. At high tide, the ocean covers it, and then backs away. It is sometimes called a salt marsh. The water from salinas can be evaporated, and useful salt is left behind. Where this is done, salinas are called salt gardens.

T is for Tektite

a scientific project in which four aquanauts live in several rooms on the ocean floor. From there they can swim out to study all kinds of life and minerals at the bottom of the sea. Of course the base has living quarters, supplies of food, and ways of keeping the air fresh. It also has laboratories in which the aquanauts can work.

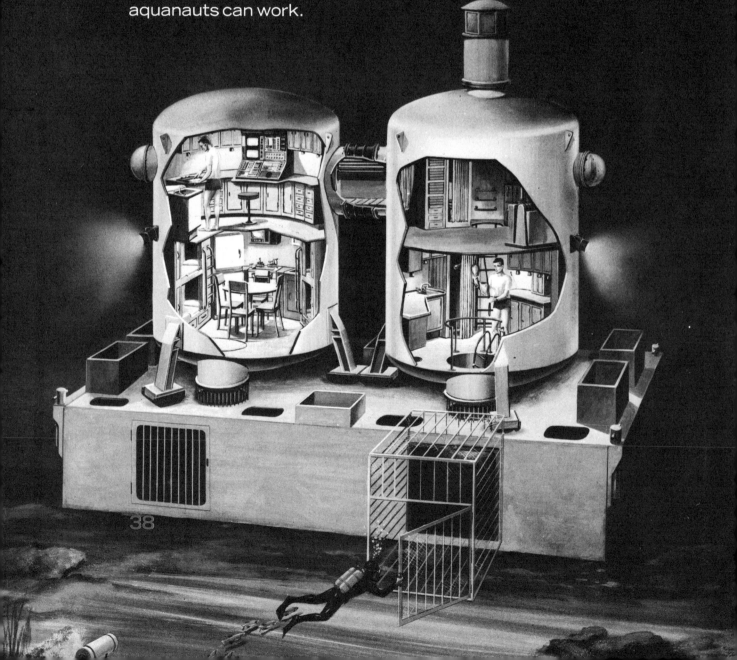

t is for tsunami (tsoo-NA-mee)

_____

_____

_____

an ocean wave caused by the sudden shock of an earthquake under the ocean floor. Such a wave is not very high in the open sea and can travel for thousands of miles without being noticed. But when it reaches the shallow water near land, the water piles up dozens of feet high. It can then do much damage. Its name comes from Japanese words that mean harbor ("tsu") and wave ("nami").

U is for Unda

_____

_____

_____

the bottom of the sea near the dry land. When waves
come in to shore, they can stir up the ocean bed where
the water is very shallow. Because the bottom is
always stirred up in this way, it is different from other
parts of the ocean floor.

U is for upwelling

_____

_____

_____

a steady upward movement of water from the deepest
part of the ocean. Creatures on the ocean surface
take in minerals from the water. When they die, they
drop to the bottom. Then their bodies break up and
give off the parts that contain those minerals.
Upwelling brings the minerals back to the surface,
where they are again used by living creatures. This
makes it possible for life on the ocean surface to continue.

41

V is for Varve

_____

_____

_____

a layer of tiny pieces of minerals which settle on the bottom of a harbor or a lake in one year. The particles put down in the summer are large. Those of the winter are dark and fine. Scientists can count the layers back for thousands of years. From the material they find, they can figure out the kinds of summers and winters there were during different times in the past.

GRAY BAND—SUMMER
DARK BAND—WINTER

—SUMMER
—WINTER
—SUMMER
—WINTER

V is for voe

_____

_____

_____

an inlet, bay, or creek. They are much alike. An inlet is a short, narrow stream that leads inland from the sea. A bay is a broader body of water with a wide opening to the sea. A creek is a small, narrow inlet or bay that goes farther inland than either of them.

W is for Whale

_____
_____
_____

the largest mammal that lives in the ocean. The sperm whale can be sixty feet long. It lives on giant squids. The blue whale can be as long as one hundred feet. It is the biggest animal that ever lived. The largest blue whales are about 150 tons, which is twice as large as the very largest kinds of dinosaurs. It has a very small throat and can eat only small forms of life, such as krill.

W is for waterspout

_____
_____
_____

a column of water drawn up from the ocean or a lake by fast-whirling air called a tornado. The water is pulled up and twisted until it looks like a funnel. This can be several hundred feet high. It can do great damage to ships and fish in its path, even though it does not last more than half an hour. If it passes over land, the water drops down at once and what is left is a tornado.

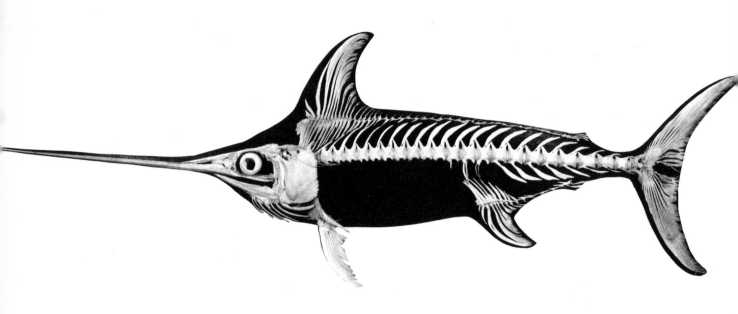

X is for Xiphius (ZIFF-ee-us)

the scientific word for swordfish. It comes from a Greek word that means sword. The swordfish has a nose that stretches out into a bill that can be five feet long. The swordfish swims fast. It is powerful and can drive its sword through the side of a wooden boat. It is also good to eat.

X is for xiphosurus (ZIFF-oh-SOOR-us)

_____

_____

_____

the scientific name of the horseshoe crab. It is from Greek words meaning swordtail, because this creature has a long, narrow tail. The horseshoe crab is not really a crab but a distant relative of spiders. Most creatures have changed over the ages, but the horseshoe crab is the same as it was in the days of the dinosaurs.

Y is for Yankee Clipper

_____

_____

_____

a kind of sailing ship that was built in the United States over a hundred years ago. It was beautiful and quiet. At that time it was the fastest way to travel across the ocean, even though the trip took several weeks. But then steamships were built which were faster transportation, so no more Yankee clippers were built.

Y is for yowling

———————————

———————————

———————————

the sound made by ice when it cracks. The edges of the breaking ice rub together and make high, screeching sounds. Scientists who study ocean ice sheets in very cold regions have to listen for strange sounds. Cracking ice can be very dangerous.

47

Z is for Zooplankton

_____

_____

_____

tiny animals that either float in surface water or swim weakly. Small shellfish and jellyfish, worms and baby fish are all zooplankton. They live on tiny plants that make up the photoplankton. Many fish, squids, and whales live on zooplankton. "Zoo" comes from a Greek word that means living being or animal.

Z is for zoogene

_____

_____

_____

parts of the ocean floor that are made up of limestone skeletons of sea creatures. Sometimes high ridges are built up of trillions of these skeletons to form reefs. Circles of zoogene that form around slowly sinking islands become round reefs or atolls.